Beware of Bad Company

Avoiding Toxic Friendships

———————

Shawn M. McBride

BEWARE OF BAD COMPANY
Copyright © 2013 by (Shawn M. McBride)

ISBN **978-1-4848-5003-9**

Dedication

This book is dedicated to the hundreds of thousands of Christian people in America—young and old—that I have been privileged to serve in various roles over the last two decades. You have been my teacher. I have been your student. You have taught me well.

To Asbury Sellers, Phil Golden, Anthony Distefano, James Lee, Jonathan Weaver, Bernard Fuller, Todd Gaston who have been the seven godly shepherds who have watched over my life from childhood until now.

To Keith Battle. You have been my mentor since the mid-90's when I met you. I admire you more than you know. No one has influenced my life and ministry to young people more than you.

Thank You

To my beautiful wife, Dana Michelle whom I have known since middle school. Your unconditional love and support for me is unmatched. You have helped me to become the man I am today. You truly are my best friend and life's companion. I love you deeply.

To my five precious children: Teshara, Jeremiah, Zachariah, Jessica-Faith and Naomi Grace. You add so much joy to my life. You are God's gift to me. Being your father is my greatest reward.

To my parents for loving me, providing for me and never giving up on me, even when I lived under your care, especially when I surrounded myself with bad company.

To David and Gloria Taylor for raising such an incredible daughter and entrusting her life to me.

To my personal administrative assistant Tiffany Dickerson for making my life flow easier every day. Thank you for faithfully and diligently taking care of the details. You make me better.

To my editorial team, I am a better speaker than I am a writer. You have given me a greater appreciation for nouns, verbs, predicates, adjectives, and the English language in general. Your expertise and skills are amazing!

Table of Contents

Introduction

You Are an Eagle, Not a Turkey!

Once upon a time there was a baby eaglet named Maurice who lived high in a nest. One day, his mother went out to cruise the skies in search of food. While she was gone, a strong wind came and knocked the baby eaglet to the ground, landing him smack dab in the midst of a turkey farm. Turkeys surrounded the stunned and confused baby eaglet. He fearfully walked around the turkey farm crying and searching for his mother.

Not long after Maurice arrived on the farm, a few of the turkeys decided to befriend and comfort the weary and hungry eaglet. One of the turkeys suggested to Maurice that he come and live with them and they would take good care of him. The lonely eaglet agreed.

As days and weeks went by, Maurice began to fit in well with his new turkey buddies, and didn't realize that he was really an eagle. Although something inside felt out of place, he ignored it and began learning to live like a turkey. He learned how to gobble like a turkey. He learned how to walk like a turkey. He even learned to dig for worms and grubs, as well as eat seeds and grains, just like a turkey. At times he would salivate and crave fresh meat, but his turkey friends convinced him that it was just part of being a turkey.

One spring morning, Maurice and the turkeys were out in an open pasture. A large eagle flying through the air caught Maurice's eye. The resemblance between Maurice and the large bird was undeniable. Maurice turned to one of his turkey friends and said, "Oh, how I wish that I could fly high above the trees and soar into the clouds like that large bird in the sky!" His turkey friend glanced skyward and quickly responded:

"Stop your dreaming! You will never be able to fly like that bird. You are just a turkey like all of us. That bird is an eagle. How many times do I have to tell you? I am a turkey, you are a turkey, our mother is a turkey, our father is a turkey, your aunt is a turkey, your uncle is a turkey, your cousins are turkeys. We are all turkeys! Got it?"

A little while later, Maurice went for a walk by himself in the woods pondering as he walked. Deep inside he knew that something was off. He was unhappy and an intense struggle was beginning to manifest. This internal battle was between what he perceived his creator had made him and the way he was living his life as he hung around the turkeys.

As he walked through the woods, he began to break down and tears ran down his beak. He knew something was not right in his life and as he felt alone and down, a wise, old owl peered down from a tree high above him.

"What's wrong, young eaglet?"

Taken aback, Maurice looked around and finally looked up.

"Hello?"

Maurice realized the owl was old and kind and felt compelled to talk to him. They spent hours just talking about what was on Maurice's mind and heart. Finally, Maurice told him about his strongest desire. He wanted to soar the clouds, hunt for game and devour fresh meat.

The owl smiled and said, "Well, just DO IT!"

Desperation and doubt clouded back in as Maurice bowed his head and said in a small voice, "I can't. I am a turkey. My mother is a turkey, my father is a turkey, my aunt is a turkey, my uncle is a turkey, my cousins are turkeys—everybody knows I come from a family of turkeys. Turkeys don't soar and eat fresh meat."

The wise owl quickly responded: "You are NOT a turkey, you are an eagle!!!"

"What are you talking about?" asked the eaglet with a perplexed look.

The owl thoughtfully responded, "Listen, I have been living in these woods a very long time, and I know an eaglet when I see one. Have you not noticed that you look different from all the other turkeys?

Have you not realized how different you feel and desire to act when you are around them?"

The wise owl continued, "Believe me young man; you are not a turkey, but an eagle. Have you ever tried to soar or eat fresh meat? Go ahead… give it a try, what do you have to lose?"

Maurice sat quietly for a moment and pondered the words of wisdom from the old owl. Slowly and carefully, for the first time in his young life, Maurice stretched out his wings, began to run, and took off for the sky. He suddenly began climbing. Higher and higher he wondered how high he could go. The higher he climbed, the happier he became. *"Yeeeees!,"* he exclaimed! *"This is so cool and natural,"* he thought as it hit him that this was who he was created to be.

As he was soaring in the clouds, he suddenly became acutely aware of another talent he had that he was never aware of. He had incredible vision! He could see the smallest details, even though he was so far from the ground. After some time, he noticed a small rabbit, moving through the grass. He circled above the rabbit, dove down, swooped his talons around the furry creature and completed his first hunt. The tension of the hunt pulsed through his veins, and the excitement of fresh meat made his mouth water. He devoured the rabbit, and he knew this was the tastiest meal he had ever eaten. *"I'll never eat grains and seeds again,"* he thought; as he relished every morsel of his fresh kill.

9

Maurice was feeling and living like he was supposed to as his natural self. He was living the way his creator intended for him to live. The longer he stayed away from the turkeys, the more focused and successful he became at soaring the skies and hunting his food.

About a week had passed and Maurice was still excited about his new discovery. He went for a visit to the farm and told his turkey friends of his new enlightenment. Of course, the turkeys tried to convince him that he was a turkey, his mother was a turkey, his father was a turkey, his aunt was a turkey, his uncle was a turkey, his cousins were turkeys, and everybody was a turkey.

Fortunately, this time he refused to believe the lie because he had discovered who he really was and he had found his purpose. At last, he bid farewell to all of his turkey friends and started out for his new journey in the skies. He was extremely overjoyed that he finally broke free from all of the turkeys that had been holding him back from living, flying, and soaring like he was created to do. Not long after, he met other eagles who continued to inspire him to be the best that he could be.

So, What's the Point?

This story primarily teaches us that whom you surround yourself with will determine the type of person you will become. When you live with turkeys, associate with turkeys, eat with turkeys, hang out with turkeys, and listen to turkeys, eventually you will begin to think and act just like a turkey, whether you intend to or not. To say it another way, the friends in your life will either be your greatest blessing, or a curse. Those whom you spend most of your time with can potentially propel your life forward, or unconsciously pull your life backwards. Having the right friends on your side will always help you to succeed, but having the wrong friends will ultimately lead to many failures and limitations on your natural talents. Thus, we must all 'Beware of Bad Company'!

With this idea in mind, there are three specific reasons that I decided to write this book.

First, for the last two decades I have had the privilege of meeting, conversing with, and serving hundreds of thousands of people as a pastor, college professor, family counselor, multi-school chaplain, national speaker, evangelist, and more recently a social media guru. I love helping people.

During this time in my own life, and through these experiences, I have discovered that some friendships can be life-giving, loving, inspiring, and very encouraging. On the other hand, some of our friendships can be draining, hurtful, and depressing.

If you are the type of person who has become dissatisfied and uncomfortable with certain friendships that have become toxic to your life, this book is for you. If you aren't sure, but your inner voice is making you question it, this book is for you.

This dissatisfaction and awareness is actually a good thing, and it is an indication that something is out of order. It is very difficult to be completely comfortable when you are in a place of dissatisfaction inside.

My hope and prayer is that this book will give you real answers about real friendships and help guide you so that you can finally get your relationships in order and set yourself on track to become who God envisions.

Secondly, it is my desire to explain to you from a negative perspective why it is critical for you to begin to disassociate yourself from the toxic turkeys that will inevitably infect you and hinder your life from soaring. You must realize that not every friendship will benefit you. Some friendships must be avoided because they are not healthy. There are certain relationships that will take away value from your life. This book is written to motivate and encourage you to walk away from those bad relationships.

Thirdly, it is my desire to teach you from a positive perspective—*like a wise owl*—how to locate the encouraging eagles that will positively affect your life and enable you to become the person that you were

12

:d to be. The positive people that we associate
re more deeply connected to us than we think.
hen we get close to positive people, whether we
e it or not, there are a variety of things that pass
and forth between them and us. Values,
ctions, morals, habits, and goals influence us
vay or another. With this knowledge, it is
rtant to realize that we can enhance our chances
coming elegant eagles by choosing the right
people with whom to develop deeper friendships.

The principles that you will discover in this book
are primarily written to encourage other youth and
young adults, however, people of all ages can benefit
from these teachings. We all are social creatures, and
are connected to people in some way.

Enjoy!

Shawn M. McBride – *Washington, DC*
www.truthforyouthamerica.org
www.shawnmcbridespeaks.com

Introduction Questions for Reflection/Discussion:

1. Maurice, the baby eaglet, accidentally ends up in a group of turkeys. Do we get involved with "turkey" friends accidentally or intentionally?

2. It's easy to dismiss the feeling that you don't quite fit with your group of friends. Is it okay to ignore these doubts?

3. What are some clues that you should separate yourself from a certain group of friends and seek a new group?

4. Do the friends you have right now drag you down, or do they encourage you?

5. Sometimes we, just like Maurice, become blind to our true abilities and talents. What is one area in which you'd like to pursue a talent and soar?

6. Whom do you seek for wise counsel?

Chapter 1
Bad Company Will Infect You
1 Corinthians 15:33 (NIV)
"Do not be misled: Bad company corrupts good character."

Many years ago, I visited a special elderly lady in the hospital and her particular illness is one that is not quickly forgotten. She had a horrible disease called gangrene, which refers to dead or dying body tissue caused by inadequate blood supply. The trademark of this terrible disease is often an infection in the body, which starts out small and gradually spreads. In her case, blood stopped flowing to her left foot because of a severe infection. As a result, her foot began to literally rot. Oh, what a horrific sight to see!

As time progressed, the disease began to overtake her foot and consequently her entire foot began decaying little by little, day by day. Typically, in situations such as this, a wise doctor would opt to completely amputate the foot so the infection would not spread throughout the entire body. Fortunately, in her case, though, they caught the gangrene infection in time and were able to treat the disease with strong medication and her foot was saved.

Although this visual is not for the light-hearted, the concept of a gangrene infection overtaking the body accurately describes what will happen to our lives if we begin to associate with bad company. Little by little, day-by-day, week-by-week, month-by-month, the infection from the lives of bad company will begin to seep into our lives. It will only be a matter of time before our lives begin to decay and rot morally, as we conform to the lives our 'friends' lead.

The Influence of Close Friends

I read a report recently that vividly highlighted the effects of bad company. Researchers from the Guttmacher Institute reported that a teenager's sexual behavior is heavily influenced by the sexual attitudes and behaviors of his or her friends.

In other words, research has now proved that young people have a greater chance of engaging in sexual intercourse if their close friends are doing so. This particular research(1) suggests:

- …The higher the proportion of a youth's friends who were sexually experienced, the greater the odds of sexual debut.
- …The odds are elevated among youth who believed they would gain their friends' respect by having sex.
- Adolescents who are highly involved with their friends may find themselves in social contexts that encourage early dating and entry into romantic relationships, which have been linked to earlier sexual initiation.
- An individual's close *circle* of friends may influence sexual debut more than a single

best friend does, possibly because an immediate network of friends is more stable over time than a specific best friend.

As people, most of us think that we are strong enough to make our own decisions and, for the most part, we are. The problem with associating with bad company is not another person will control us, but how two key areas deep within us change: influence and perspective.

It is impossible to live in this world and not be infected by other people at some point. Certain friends have the power to influence us, our choices, and the decisions we make on a daily basis. Furthermore, their attitudes and actions will shape our perspective (our view of what is right or wrong) and shape our decisions in a positive or negative way.

Do Not Be Misled

The Apostle Paul, who wrote *1 Corinthians 15:33* (NIV), started the verse with these four critical words; *"DO NOT BE MISLED."* I believe this was meant as a warning to keep us aware of our company.

- DO NOT BE MISLED means that you should never think you are incapable of being infected by bad company.
- DO NOT BE MISLED teaches that you should never underestimate the power and influence of bad company.

- DO NOT BE MISLED suggests that you should not fool yourself into thinking that you are different, or are an exception to the rule.

We all have the tendency, like anyone else, to eventually be infected by the people we choose to be close to. This tendency is especially strong if you are a young person, because most young people are seeking approval, and possibly attention, from others. Often times, the hormones of adolescence skew our good judgment, make us feel invincible, and prohibit us from realizing that we must live with our actions for the rest of our lives. This becomes especially difficult when faced with pressure from our friends.

One would think that bad company could simply be tolerated and ignored. Not so! You see, after investing time in toxic friendships, your life will eventually become sick. If you are not careful and cautious, you will begin to pick up the negative behaviors and patterns of the people around you— often unintentionally. The longer you are around bad company, the more desensitized you become to the sins they commit. Before long, you will be tempted to use their vulgar language, laugh at their inappropriate jokes, feed into their hurtful criticisms, and begin to gossip about others, or copy their negative or perverted behaviors, whatever they may be. What once would bother you will intrigue you and be accepted as normal. After all, bad company does not make you change your ways; it simply changes your moral *perspective,* which leads to a gradual downward spiral of your own moral behavior. Do Not Be Misled!

Dear readers, no matter how strong you are, you must be careful with whom you form relationships. Bad company will adversely affect your walk with Christ and your witness to the people around you. Perhaps a time of reflection may be needed. You may need to step back, distance yourself from certain people, and begin to evaluate your relationships and your circle of friends. This process is extremely difficult and is like having major surgery, but the benefits far outweigh the risks.

What makes this process so difficult is realizing that some of our closest friends might just be the *"bad company"* in our lives. Even though you may enjoy their company, these types of relationships must be amputated. Sadly, unlike gangrene, there is no physical medicine available that can cure a corrupt soul.

Today's Tweet:

@shawnmcbride74

If you lay down with dogs, you will get up with fleas!

#bewareofbadcompany

Chapter 1 Questions for Reflection/Discussion:

1. Imagine you have a deep cut on your thumb that becomes infected. How does it look? How does it feel? How does it affect your use of that thumb?

2. In what ways can a friendship become infected?

3. Peer pressure influences us—good and bad. Do you think peer pressure effects you in more positive or negative ways?

4. How much do your friends shape your perspective and decisions?

5. Why do you think the Apostle Paul included the phrase "Do not be misled" in *1 Corinthians 15:33*?

6. *Bad company corrupts good character.* How would you define "corrupt"? Describe a typical sequence of how this corruption might occur.

7. What's one specific situation you have been in where you underestimated the power of bad company?

8. Are there certain people you need to seriously consider distancing yourself from?

Chapter 2
Death by Association

Proverbs 22:24–25 (NIV)
"Do not make friends with a hot-tempered
person.
Do not associate with one easily-angered,
or you may learn their ways
and get yourself ensnared."

The death of anyone is a tragedy, but the death of a famous person brings true shock to masses of people simultaneously. Between 2009 and 2012, there were several celebrities whose untimely deaths caught my attention and had me scratching my head. The following celebrities all died sudden and unexpected deaths:

- Michael Jackson: *June 25, 2009*
- Amy Winehouse, *July 23, 2011*
- Whitney Houston, *February 11, 2012*

When the tragic stories of each of these celebrities broke in the national media, there was a great sense of shock and disbelief all over the world. Many asked, "Why?" We often seem to idolize celebrities and they seem to have it all, so what could go wrong and how could they suddenly be gone? Sadly, these three individuals all seemed to die before their time.

I would like to suggest to you that the handwriting was on the wall for all three of these individuals simply because of the associations they kept. Their downfall can be specifically traced back to the choices they made to forge associations with the wrong people.

Celebrity	Their Associations
Michael Jackson	Dr. Conrad Murray was a close associate of Michael Jackson and became his personal physician. He was found guilty of involuntary manslaughter in November 2011.
Amy Winehouse	Blake Fielder-Civil is the ex-husband of Amy Winehouse. Blake publicly admitted and acknowledged that he originally introduced Amy to hard drugs, which led to alcohol abuse and her death.
Whitney Houston	For years, rumor had it that Bobby Brown had introduced Whitney Houston to drugs – but Michael Houston, one of the singer's two older brothers, revealed to Oprah Winfrey that the real story was quite different. He took full responsibility.

This list can go on and on, but the key point is that I believe Michael, Amy, and Whitney would still be alive and entertaining us today, if it were not for their associations. The bad company they kept played a strong role in their lifestyles, and ultimately, their deaths.

The following graphic can be used to help us when thinking about our friendships and associates.

Two Types of Associations

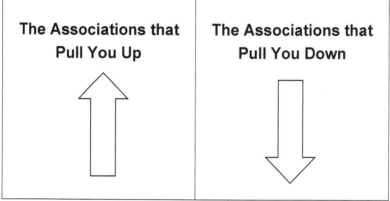

The Associations that Pull You Up	The Associations that Pull You Down

I love the wisdom shared by former Army General, Colin Powell, in his book, *My American Journey*:

"The less you associate with certain people, the more your life will improve. Anytime you tolerate mediocrity in others, it increases your mediocrity. An important attribute in successful people is their impatience with negative thinking and negative acting people. As you grow, your associates will change. Some of your friends will not want to go on. They will want you to stay where you are. Friends that don't help you climb, will want you to crawl.

Your friends will stretch your vision or choke your dream. Those that don't increase you will eventually decrease you."

(Colin Powell–My American Journey)(2)

If you have friends (associates) in your life who pull you up, then you should give thanks and take every opportunity you can to enjoy their company. It is wise to spend as much time as possible with people who make you a better person and help you grow.

On the other hand, *Proverbs 22:24–25* warns us not to "make friends" or even "associate" with certain people because their effect on our lives over time can be disastrous and ultimately pull us down. The writer gives us this warning because he understands that it is only a matter of time before we 'learn their ways', and ultimately become 'ensnared.' As I have stated before, this is not always an intentional change and we often think we can overcome it, but nobody is immune to this particular social pitfall.

Recently, counselors were at a local high school near where I live just outside of Washington, DC, to speak with students after a female senior was found dead. Her name was Michelle. She was only age 17 and was an incredible varsity student athlete.

Unfortunately, according to police, Michelle tragically died in a murder-suicide involving an angry man she met during recruitment to the U.S. Army Reserves. The detectives believe that the man she was involved with was almost twice her age. He ultimately shot her, and then himself, inside his home.

It is my understanding that Army recruiters are barred from having personal relationships with their recruits. Apparently, this rule was violated. What's even more startling is that Michelle's parents were unaware of the relationship she was having with this man. My friends, if you feel the need to hide your associations that should be your first red flag of many that you are in bad company.

The message of this chapter cannot be any clearer. If you choose to associate with destructive people, you will eventually get hurt. You must pay careful attention to your friends. If you associate with, or surround yourself with the wrong people, they will negatively impact your life and drive you off course.

Today's Tweet:

@shawnmcbride74
Michael Jackson died an untimely death because of
Dr. Conrad Murray. Bad company can kill you.
#bewareofbadcompany

Chapter 2 Questions for Reflection/Discussion:

1. What other tragic celebrity deaths can you think of? Were these individuals associating with the wrong type of people?

2. Think about the graphic in this chapter with the up and down arrows. Which arrow is bigger and stronger for you—the one pulling you up or the one pulling you down?

3. Colin Powell said, "*Anytime you tolerate mediocrity in others, it increases your mediocrity.*" Why do you agree or disagree?

4. Consider Powell's further statement, "*Some of your friends will not want to go on. They will want you to stay where you are. Friends that don't help you climb will want you to crawl.*" How would you describe this kind of friend?

5. Who is one friend that pulls you up? Be thankful for this person.

6. Think of one friend who pulls you down. Are you becoming ensnared? Should you consider separating yourself from him/her?

7. Are you in a relationship that you are hiding from others? Why are you keeping it hidden?

Chapter 3
7 Characteristics of Foolish Friends
Proverbs 14:7 (NIV)
"Stay away from a fool, for you will not find knowledge on their lips."

I recently purchased and began to read the autobiography of legendary NFL quarterback, Michael Vick. His story gripped me and put into perspective the very reason I am writing this book.

> *"A lot of my poor choices and subsequent mistakes can be attributed mostly to two things: my weak resolve in telling people no, and the people I chose to be associated with. I had an entourage of pretty questionable characters… I was surrounded by them all of the time whenever I was not playing football… It was my decision to have that entourage, and it wasn't a good one. It was the first in a series of bad decisions… The Falcons had concerns about the people I was hanging around, but I don't believe team officials knew the extent of what I was doing until it was too late." (Vick, Finally Free p 86)(3).*

As Michael Vick's story demonstrates, his decision to hang out with foolish friends ultimately ruined his life.

His example should teach us that the more time you spend with foolish people, the more their folly will begin to seep into your life and taint you. Their faulty navigational system will eventually steer you off course.

7 Characteristics of Foolish Friends
Proverbs 6:16–19 (NLT)

"There are six things the LORD hates – no, seven things he detests: haughty eyes, a lying tongue, hands that kill the innocent, a heart that plots evil, feet that race to do wrong, a false witness who pours out lies, a person who sows discord in a family."

As we navigate through life and encounter people each day, we should keep a watchful eye out for certain negative characteristics. Whenever we see these characteristics in a person, red flags should go up, and we should make a point not to forge deep friendships. An old saying is that we become like the five people we are around most. Make certain that your top five do not possess the following characteristics:

1. Haughty Eyes (Arrogant / Prideful Friends)

This refers to someone with a stuck-up attitude of superiority, as if they are the best thing since sliced bread. This person is on a high horse and looks down on others. It is an attitude where the person acts as if: *"I am a winner, but you are a loser;" "I am better than you;" "I am smart and you are dumb;" "I am strong and you are weak;" "I am a Democrat, but you are a Republican;" "I look good, but you look ugly;"* etc. Such pride and arrogance is always denounced throughout the entire Bible.

2. A Lying Tongue (Lying Friends)

This describes a person who is dishonest and loose with truth. They are deceivers because they willingly make false statements. They are shady, exaggerate stories, hide reality, and break trust. The primary reason this person lies is to avoid consequences, or to be accepted by their peers.

Make friends with this kind of person and sooner or later you will be deceived or betrayed by them. It is inevitable.

When we befriend people who are not honest, we run the risk of eventually becoming dishonest ourselves.

If you are close to people who are always covering things up, lying to their parents/spouse/friends about where they have been, what they have been doing, or where they are going, this behavior will eventually begin to rub off on you.

3. Hands That Shed Innocent Blood (Friends Who Take Advantage of Others)

The phrase "innocent blood" appears in the Bible 17 times, with only one of those occurrences in the New Testament. *(Matthew 27:4)*. It is a reference to murder and the killing of innocent people. It speaks to taking the life of an innocent person.

While you may not be best friends with a mass murderer, I suspect that the principle applied in this verse covers more than the physical shedding of blood. In my opinion, there are many ways to hurt innocent people.

We shed innocent blood every time we encourage a friend to devalue the life of another human being, or an unborn child through an abortion. It happens whenever we bully someone, or who takes advantage of people who are vulnerable, powerless, and cannot fend for themselves. We shed innocent blood when we get close to people who have an extreme and total disregard for the lives of others who have been created in the image of God.

4. A Heart That Plots Evil (Scheming Friends)

This describes a person who can, without a guilty conscience, design, scheme and implement illegal and destructive activity. It speaks of the kind of person who can justify doing any kind of wrong, as long as they don't get caught. Do not get connected with these slippery characters. Keep your distance. Hooking up with these types of people will spell disaster.

5. Feet That Race To Do Wrong (Friends Eager To Do Wrong)

This describes a person who is excited, eager, and passionate about doing wrong. Rather than resisting the temptations of life, they run towards wrongdoing and are anxious for the next sinful and illegal activity. These fools have a heart that is inclined toward doing evil, instead of doing good.

6. A False Witness Who Utters Lies (Gossiping Friends)

This type of person is similar to the person I mentioned previously who is dishonest, however, the red flag in this verse is being raised against a specific form of lying: *a false witness.* A false witness is a person that uses their words to slander others.

This kind of person speaks malicious words, spreads rumors, and is quick to damage others with their words. They are unable to keep secrets and confidential information to themselves because they want to expose someone.

This type of person is careless with their words and seeks to tear down other people with the intent to ruin their reputation. This type of friend cannot keep things confidential and private. They are gossips. You cannot talk freely with this person because they will tell it all to everyone! This is not a safe person to get close to. Steer clear and run in the opposite direction fast. A good rule of thumb is to remember that if this type of person will gossip TO you, they will also gossip ABOUT you.

7. A Person Who Sows Discord in a Family

Another way of saying this is a person who spreads strife and causes conflict among people. They seem to hate peace and unity, and in the words of my oldest daughter, are always "starting stuff." This person is always full of drama. They are haters. They have the ability to make a difficult situation worse by spewing poisonous words.

These are the seven characteristics to watch for when developing friendships, but I must make a crucial point. God teaches us to LOVE others.

Therefore, staying away from foolish people does not mean they are insignificant, or that we are better than they are! We should always be kind to them, serve them, love them, and encourage them. However, it does mean that we will not invite them to walk closely with us through our lives. It means that we will not give them a position of influence in our lives. It means that we choose to take a pass if they are bent on demonstrating these characteristics and living these negative types of lifestyles.

Today's Tweet:

@shawnmcbride74

Michael Vick went 2 prison because of D.A.W.G.S not
D.O.G.S. Hanging with fools will ruin u
#bewareofbadcompany

Chapter 3 Questions for Reflection/Discussion:

1. Why do you think people like Michael Vick often have an "entourage" of questionable friends?

2. Who are the five people you are around the most? Are these people that you want to be like?

3. Why do you suppose "haughty eyes," or pride, is listed first in the verse of what God hates?

4. We know lying is wrong. But how about simply saying nothing—not speaking up with the truth?

5. Think of several ways you have seen innocent people being taken advantage of. What are some subtle ways you devalue others?

6. If you have a friend who is "plotting evil," what should you do?

7. Gossip is tantalizing… but so destructive. What specific steps can you take to change—both as a listener and as a spreader—of gossip?

8. How can you balance loving a person as God teaches, without keeping them as a close friend?

Chapter 4
Leave Lot Alone!

Country music singer, Taylor Swift, had a popular song titled: *"I Knew You Were Trouble"*. In this hit, Taylor is feeling anger and regret because she was recovering after getting herself involved with a person who caused her a lot of *trouble*, hence the title of the song. Throughout the song, she continued to refer to the person as *"trouble, trouble, trouble. Oh, oh, trouble, trouble, trouble."* She openly suggested that it was totally her own fault. She references being played, feeling shame, and how she cried as she sat on the cold, hard ground. Oh Trouble!

How relevant to our lives! This song serves as a great example of what can happen when we let the wrong type of people in. It ultimately leads to TROUBLE and WE end up hurt because we realize that we are responsible for whom we allow to be a significant part of our lives. This is why it is so important to be aware and reflective of our relationships with others.

One of the most powerful examples I can illustrate for you concerning troublesome company is found in my favorite book, *The Bible,* from the life of Abram. This story is simple, yet profound, because Abram's life was often full of trouble due to his connection with his nephew, named Lot. Although Lot was a relative, he was bad company for Abram for many different reasons.

Genesis 12:1–4 (NIV)

"The LORD had said to Abram, "Go from your country, your people and your father's household to the land I will show you.² I will make you into a great nation, and I will bless you; will make your name great, and you will be a blessing.³ I will bless those who bless you, and whoever curses you I will curse; and all peoples on earth will be blessed through you."⁴ So Abram went, as the LORD had told him; and <u>Lot went with him</u>."

You see, the Lord had a specific purpose and plan for Abram's life. He was about to take him to a whole new level, but in order for Abram to fulfill this purpose, God asked him to be separated from his region and relatives.

Now, this seems to be an odd request, so you might wonder why Abram needed to be separated from his relatives. Apparently, many of the people of Abram's region, including his relatives, were not worshippers of the one true God. History teaches us that they were polytheistic, which means that they worshipped many different gods, not the true God. Thus, the Lord's intent was to move Abram completely away from that region and those relatives, into an entirely new environment where He would work through Abram's life and fulfill His will.

According to verse 4, Abram only followed half of the instructions that were given to him. He left his region, but not a particular relationship. How do I know this? Notice the four important words at the end of verse four: *"Lot went with him"*. The very fact that Abram took Lot with him for the journey only complicated matters. As we later learn in the book of Genesis, Lot's life and Abram's life were in stark contrast. Abram was a godly, righteous man and Lot was very worldly and carnal. As we have learned before, bad company will inevitably bring strife to our lives, and even Abram's life could not escape this.

As we continue to read, specifically in chapters 13 and following in Genesis, we see that the relationship Abram shared with Lot was very toxic indeed:

Genesis 13:5–7 (NIV)
"Now Lot, who was moving about with Abram, also had flocks and herds and tents. 6 But the land could not support them while they stayed together, for their possessions were so great that they were not able to stay together. 7 And quarreling arose between Abram's herders and Lot's. The Canaanites and Perizzites were also living in the land at that time."

Notice the two phrases in verse six:
"...while they stayed together"

"...they were not able to stay together."

Genesis 13:8–9 (NIV)

"So Abram said to Lot, "Let's not have any quarreling between you and me, or between your herders and mine, for we are close relatives. ⁹ Is not the whole land before you? Let's part company. If you go to the left, I'll go to the right; if you go to the right, I'll go to the left."

Notice the phrase:

"Let's part company."

Separation Is Key

The Bible teaches us a very important lesson through Abram's life. The point that I want you to take away from this is that some people simply cannot go with you to the place and level that the Lord desires to take you. Some people will cause your life more harm than good. You must identify the *'Lots'* in your life and separate from them as much as you can. Leave them alone!

Someone once told me that the definition of insanity is dealing with the same person over and over again and expecting them to act differently this time. This likely will not happen. *Separation is key.*

The first step to having healthy relationships is to identify the toxic relationships in your life. Unfortunately, sometimes these relationships can be our close friends, or as in Abram's situation, a member of our family. This makes separation extremely difficult on us physically and emotionally.

The number one reason that holds most people back from eliminating troublesome people from their lives is *guilt*. We think that we are being rude or mean by not associating with the toxic person, or we worry too much about how they will feel instead of the damage they are causing or the bad influence they are having on those around them.

Friends, remember God calls us to walk with love. Therefore, we should continue to love and be kind, but we can minimize these relationships through the one key word of this chapter: SEPARATION.

Another point to remember is that just because you have decided you want a change in your life doesn't mean the *'Lots'* in your life want to do the same. While it might not be possible to completely get rid of all the *'Lots'* in your life, minimizing contact with them, or avoiding them, can really make the difference in your own well being.

Perhaps you may need to take drastic steps to close yourself off from these people completely so that you can move on with your life and become a stronger and better person. Separation might involve giving the relationship a break for 40 days, ignoring phone calls/text messages, deleting friends off social media networks, blocking e-mails, breaking up, going separate ways, or even moving out if you are living with that person. We simply must weed some people out of our lives if we want to move forward in a positive direction.

Trying to change how people behave is a waste of time and energy, but making sure to surround yourself with friends and family who have a righteous, sunny, simple, and uplifting disposition and with whom you can be yourself, is a great way of making sure you become the best version of you that you can be!

Sometimes, we must step away from a relationship in order to see it for what it really is. One of the most amazing things that will happen when you break free from the *'Lots'* in your life, is how you will begin to feel once some time has elapsed. In my years of counseling others, people have shared with me that they began to wonder what they had ever seen in their *'Lots'* in the first place. When you are deeply entrenched in a relationship, you cannot see a *'Lot'*. This is called a blind spot because you are so close to the situation that it hinders your ability to be objective about the relationship.

Genesis 13:14–17 (NIV)
"The Lord said to Abram <u>after Lot had parted from him</u>, "Look around from where you are, to the north and south, to the east and west. All the land that you see, I will give to you and your offspring forever. 16 I will make your offspring like the dust of the earth, so that if

anyone could count the dust, then your offspring could be counted. 17 Go, walk through the length and breadth of the land, for I am giving it to you."

Notice the phrase:
"The Lord said to Abram after Lot had parted from him…"

It was not until the relationship was severed and disconnected that the Lord could freely speak to Abram and bless his life.

Today's Tweet:

@shawnmcbride74
Surround yourself with people who show signs of GENIUS. Avoid people who show signs of STUPIDITY. #bewareofbadcompany

Chapter 4 Questions for Reflection/Discussion:

1. What song title would describe a relationship you are struggling with right now?

2. At times, relationships can definitely hurt. Why do they hurt so badly?

3. In the verses in Genesis about Abram and Lot, why do you think Abram allowed Lot to come with him?

4. Did you notice that not only did Abram and Lot take part in quarreling, but "quarreling arose between Abram's herders and Lot's?" When have you experienced a disagreement between two people that spread to others?

5. Is there a toxic person in your life that you need to separate yourself from this week?

6. Is this person someone you can still show love to while you are minimizing contact? Or, do you need to totally separate yourself from them?

7. Who is the one person you can most be yourself with?

8. Do you feel connected or disconnected to God?

Chapter 5
You Make Me Sick

Psalm 26:4–5 (TNIV)
"I do not sit with the deceitful,
nor do I associate with hypocrites.
⁵ I abhor the assembly of evildoers
and refuse to sit with the wicked."

The Bible teaches us that we should not spend most of our time with the deceitful, hypocritical, evil, or wicked of the world. Unfortunately, sometimes we are already in such close relationships with these types of people that we have a hard time determining who they are. A simple reflection of our relationships should guide us in the right direction of identifying unhealthy connections.

There are six characteristics that will help you to identify unhealthy relationships:

1. **Unhealthy relationships take away from you more than they give to you.**

   Good relationships should always be a win/win situation. The relationship should be *mutually* beneficial. Friendships should always flow in two directions. Entering into a relationship with someone based only on how the relationship will benefit the other person is not wise.

   For example, if you are in a relationship with a person and they are always talking

46

about themselves, or if you are constantly giving your friends advice, help, encouragement, a listening ear, and support, but they are not providing the same support back to you, you are in an unhealthy relationship. Also, if you have the feeling that you are "chasing" the other person in order to make the relationship work, and they are not placing the same value on the friendship as you, the relationship is out of balance and cannot survive.

2. **Unhealthy relationships drain your physical, mental, and emotional energy.**

One of the best ways to know if you are in an unhealthy relationship is to assess how you feel. When you are with this person, do you feel better or worse about yourself and your life? When you spend time together, do you feel uplifted, relaxed, and confident or do you feel depressed, nervous, unsure, and confused? When you are away from this person, do you feel certain and at peace about your relationship, or do you feel doubtful and anxious about it? If you feel like the latter half of these comparative questions, more often than not, you may be in a toxic relationship. If your intuition, or gut feeling, is telling you that something is not right, don't ignore it!

3. Unhealthy relationships are verbally and emotionally abusive.

If you are in any type of relationship with someone and they are saying bad things about you, or making you feel bad about yourself, you are not in a healthful or normal relationship. This sometimes happens in a girlfriend/boyfriend situation due to control issues, or in a 'friendship' due to jealousy, or even among family members.

As an example of this, not long ago, there was a young lady, whom I'll call Sabrina, who was struggling with relationship trouble caused by two close relatives. They were making her life miserable by demeaning her, belittling her, disregarding her, degrading her, and ultimately devaluing her. She felt as if she were being treated like a piece of dirt because she was constantly being talked about behind her back and undermined by them. From her perspective, she was trying desperately to make the relationship work because they were relatives, but she constantly was rebuffed, rejected, and unloved. This relationship was toxic to her well-being and is a clear example of where separation, as much as possible, would be needed.

4. Unhealthy relationships encourage you to behave in ways that are against your beliefs and morals.

The fact that we begin to act like those that we associate with is proven time and time again in the world around us. Each of us is raised with our own value system and set of beliefs, or morals. You know what you feel is right or wrong. If you are in a relationship with a person where you often feel tempted or feel your value system shifting negatively, this is extremely dangerous to your own character.

Relationships should always lift you up and make you a better person. If they don't, separate before it is too late!

5. Unhealthy relationships bring out the absolute worst feelings in you.

Unhealthy people will make you feel uncomfortable, without saying anything. They tend to be judgmental, so whenever you are around them, you feel like you're on trial. For whatever reason, when you are around them, you might feel awkward and insecure.

Somehow, they have the ability to intentionally, and sometimes unintentionally, pour water on your dreams and make sure to give you a endless negative reasons why your dreams will never happen. They tend to be

49

'*downers*' and simply see the dark side of life, whereas you see the sun shining bright like a diamond. You are positive, but they are negative. Complaining about everyone and everything is constant and second nature for them. They see their glass as always half empty, rather than half full.

6. **Unhealthy people are manipulative and leave you feeling guilty, incompetent, and confused.**

Friends, this is a very important characteristic! Many of us tend to be a bit naïve when it comes to this one. Often, toxic individuals struggle with accepting responsibility for their own actions and have mastered the art of manipulation. This means they have a powerful way of turning certain situations around on you, which ultimately leads to you feeling guilty and shameful, when in essence, you are not to blame. This is another situation where they leave you feeling confused and frustrated because they are such eloquent smooth-talkers and twisters of the truth. It makes them feel better about themselves if they turn situations around and place the blame on you.

An important point is that not every toxic relationship will exhibit all six characteristics, but if any of these negative traits show up in your relationship that is a relationship you will need to evaluate and keep a close eye on.

I leave you with this simple graphic that will help you in evaluating your connections with others:

Healthy Relationships	Unhealthy Relationships
Fuel your life	Are toxic / poisonous
Make you confident	Tear you down
Help you feel relaxed	Feed your fears
Encourage good decisions	Waste your time
Build you up	Drain your energy
Help you grow in your faith	Reduce effectiveness
Encourage your life	Sap your resources
Infuse you with joy	Will lie to you
Lift you up	Are critical of you
Strengthen you	Encourage bad choices
A honest with you	Foster negative thinking
Inspire you	Make you depressed

Today's Tweet:

@shawnmcbride74

A bad relationship is like bad movie. U won't leave
because u hope the next scene will get better
#bewareofbadcompany

Chapter 5 Questions for Reflection/Discussion:

1. Overall, would you say most of your relationships are healthy or unhealthy?

2. What one relationship of yours is the most mutually beneficial? How do you feel about that person?

3. Are you in a one-sided relationship right now? How do you know it's out of balance?

4. What should you do if you are the one constantly giving in a relationship?

5. Have you thought about your value system? What three aspects are most important to you in any relationship?

6. Are you around a judgmental person? How do you—and how should you—handle interactions with that person?

7. Manipulative people can poison friendships. Look carefully at yourself—do you sometimes manipulate those around you?

8. Think about one relationship you have that might be unhealthy. Go through the chart at the end of the chapter to evaluate it more carefully.

Chapter 6
Building Your Championship Team

Proverbs 13:20 (NIV)
"Walk with the wise and become wise,
for a companion of fools suffers harm."

A few years ago, NBA superstar and future hall-of-famer, LeBron James, announced his decision to leave the Cleveland Cavaliers on national television. This decision came after being a star player for seven seasons. He made the choice to take his talents to south Miami to become a player for the Heat. According to LeBron, the reason he decided to leave was plain and simple:

"It is going to give me the best opportunity to win, and win for multiple years... I want to win championships... "

In a nutshell, LeBron was saying "If I am going to WIN, I must surround myself with the team that gives me the best chance of WINNING." His decision eventually paid off. A couple of years later, his team won the national championship.

This same mentality is true for the friends that we choose. If we are going to WIN in life, we must decide to surround ourselves with the people that give us the best chance of WINNING. Choosing the right friends is like putting together our own championship dream team. If we choose wisely, it will greatly increase our chances of being successful.

Before we put together your official roster, I think it is important to understand the meaning of **Proverbs 13:20:**

> *"Walk with the wise and become wise,*
> *for a companion of fools suffers harm."*

This verse is teaching that surrounding ourselves with wise friends will inevitably make us wise. On the contrary, associating with fools will eventually bring us trouble.

It is important to note that the word *wise* used in this verse does NOT only refer to intelligence. It also refers to someone who has a "skill for living," particularly in the sense of making good choices and decisions. In comparison to the wise person, a fool is not necessarily a person who is ignorant or unintelligent. Rather, the fool willingly resists and rebels against what he / she knows to be right, and insists on stubbornly doing his / her own will.

When building your winning team, it is important to surround yourself with people who have the same values, or better values, than yourself. In this way, we are making ourselves better people. Also, think about the life goals you have for yourself and seek individuals who have obtained those life goals themselves, or who have a similar life goal and are making successful strides towards this goal. These people will be wise from experience and will be able to help you meet your goals.

The graphic on the following page will be useful in helping you find people who complement your goals in life.

Cause and Effect

I Desire	I Must
More wisdom	Hang out with wise people.
Better grades	Surround myself with honor roll students.
Stronger convictions / values	Associate with peers who have strong convictions and values.
More money	Seek out people that have honest financial success.
More kindness	Befriend people who treat others with kindness.
Sexual abstinence	Get close to people who have made a commitment to abstain and to save themselves.
A drug free life	Chill with people who say NO to drugs.
Clean language	Become companions with folks who do not like using vulgar language.

YOUR TEAM ROSTER

Keep the following guidelines in mind when building your WINNING team:

1. **Consult older people who are wise**.

It is always wise to ask the advice of those who have a "skill for living." This is very difficult for many of us. To the younger generation, elders may seem feeble, old-fashioned, and out of style. However, they possess something extremely valuable that we can benefit from: WISDOM, gained through EXPERIENCE. The actions of King Rehoboam in the following scripture serve to remind us why we should always consider the advice of our elders.

1 Kings 12:6–7 (NIV)

"Then King Rehoboam consulted the elders who had served his father Solomon during his lifetime. "How would you advise me to answer these people?" he asked. They replied, "If today you will be a servant to these people and serve them and give them a favorable answer, they will always be your servants."

1 Kings 12 teaches us that Solomon, the king of Israel, had died. His son, Rehoboam, became the king and was struggling over the immediate decisions he had to make. As a result, King Rehoboam sought the advice of the older, experienced people who advised his own father, Solomon, during his lifetime.

These older people were intelligent and ultimately had a ton of experience in handling critical issues within the kingdom. These senior advisors also knew both Solomon and Rehoboam. They understood the society they lived in and suggested to the king that if he showed kindness and a servant's heart to the people, they would love and serve him forever. They were telling him to serve the people in their best interests, respond to their needs, and speak good words to them, and he would become a successful king, just like his deceased father.

I applaud Rehoboam because he was humble enough to ask for help. It takes a lot of humility to admit that we don't know everything and to make ourselves teachable so we can learn from others. Proud and arrogant people think they are wiser than others and seldom take advice.

2. Be careful about listening to your inexperienced peers.
1 Kings 12:8–11 (NIV)

"Rehoboam rejected the advice the elders gave him and consulted the young men who had grown up with him. 9 He asked them, "What is your advice? How should we answer these people who say to me, 'Lighten the yoke

your father put on us'?"10 The young men who had grown up with him replied, "These people have said to you, 'Your father put a heavy yoke on us, but make our yoke lighter.' Now tell them, 'My little finger is thicker than my father's waist. 11 My father laid on you a heavy yoke; I will make it even heavier. My father scourged you with whips; I will scourge you with scorpions."

Going to the elders for advice was a very good decision on the part of King Rehoboam. Unfortunately, he did not listen to his elders. It appears that even before Rehoboam ever consulted with the younger men, he had already rejected their advice. His youthful friends offered him the exact opposite advice than the elders. These young friends told Rehoboam what he already wanted to do. He, in essence, followed the instructions from his immature and inexperienced peers who would tell him what he WANTED to hear rather than what he NEEDED to hear. Bad move!

3. **Consider the consequences of your decisions.**

Listening to bad advice will always lead to bad results. Therefore, we must consider the advice we are given carefully. Hip-hop sensation, Frank Ocean, asks an important question in a popular radio song: *"Or, do you not think so far ahead?"* This question is brilliant and is precisely what needs to happen whenever you are seeking advice. THINK FAR AHEAD! That is, you should always consider the <u>consequences</u> and <u>outcomes</u> of your decision.

When making decisions, you should always ask yourself questions such as:

1. What will the effects of my decision mean?
2. What will happen if I listen to the older and wise people, who have experience with this?
3. What will happen if I listen to my peers?
4. What's the worst potential outcome from my actions?

Next, evaluate your answers to these questions to make the BEST decision.

Rehoboam did not think far ahead about the consequences of his decision. Because he did not take heed to the good advice he was given by the wise elders, the results were tragic. As the story continued, civil war broke out in Israel, which opened the door to four hundred years of strife, and eventually, the destruction of the entire nation. This story serves to prove that listening to bad advice will always bring you bad results. Be careful when listening to the inexperience of youth, versus the wisdom of the mature. An important point is not to just choose the advice that is the easiest, or most pleasing, without thinking through the situation maturely.

I suspect that, just like Rehoboam, you have older, wiser people in your life who are willing to offer you good advice. Perhaps these people are your parents, teachers, close relatives, or even a mentor. This story teaches us that we should always seek out and listen to advice from wise and godly people. The wise people will encourage you to do what's right, and tell you the things you need to hear, even if you don't like them. Sometimes, the cool and hip younger crowd will lead you in the wrong direction. I don't believe this happens intentionally, but is often the result from the lack of life experience. Finally, always consider the outcomes of your decisions.

Today's Tweet:

@shawnmcbride74
The fastest way 2 change yourself is 2 hang out with the people who are already the way you want to be #bewareofbadcompany

Chapter 6 Questions for Reflection/Discussion:

1. Have you been part of a winning team? What caused that particular team to win?

2. What five qualities would you use to describe someone who is wise?

3. Look back at the "Cause and Effect" chart in this chapter. What else do *you* really desire—either right now or in the future? Add that to the left column. List the corresponding action(s) in the right column.

4. Now rank the items in the chart, from most the important to you to the least important. What is the most important goal on your list?

5. Who is one older person you know that has a "skill for living" and could be a source of good advice to achieve your goal?

6. Why do you think King Rehoboam consulted the elders if he was just going to ignore their advice?

7. Do you ask for help? Whom do you ask?

8. When have you followed bad advice? What happened?

Chapter 7
Three Levels of Friendships

Proverbs 27:17 (NIV)
"As iron sharpens iron, so one person sharpens another."

When I was 10 years old, a popular hip-hop group called Whodini released a song that would become one of the most played songs during that year. The song was called "Friends." The words of the song are as follows:

Friends... How many of us have them?
Friends... Ones we can depend on.
Friends... How many of us have them?
Friends... Before we go any further, let's be Friends!
'Friends' is a word we use every day.
Most the time we use it in the wrong way.
Now you can look the word up, again and again.
But, the dictionary doesn't know the meaning of friends.
And, if you ask me, you know, I couldn't be much help.
Because a friend is somebody you judge for yourself.
Some are ok, and they treat you real cool.
But, some mistake kindness for being a fool.
We like to be with some, because they're funny.
Others come around when they need some

money.
Some you grew up with, around the way.
And you're still real close to this very day
Homeboys through the summer, winter, spring and fall.
And, then there's some we wish we never knew at all.
And this list goes on, again and again.
But these are the people that we call friends."

This song stands out to me because it accurately describes the different levels of friendships we hold. Think of all the people you have contact with each day, week, month, and year. We have a multitude of connections with those around us! Thus, not all of our friendships are created equal. The friendships we have can be divided into three different levels, depending on the closeness of our relationships.

Outer Circle of Friends

- Includes acquaintances—These people come and go in and out of your life. It includes people who recognize us, and we recognize them, whether or not we remember each other's names.

- Includes weekday friends—We see them regularly at school, extra-curricular activities, or work. This group includes select teammates and friendly neighbors.

- Includes social media friends—We know who they are, and some basic facts about them, but we may not see them often.

- We are nice to these people as we cross paths throughout our daily lives. We may engage in small talk with them.

When we make friends with someone, they always begin in this Outer Circle of Friendship. Thus, it is the largest circle of friends, because we do not have close relationships with these individuals. When friends are in this outer layer, it is easier for us to be objective and 'see them for who they really are' because we have not developed close attachments to them. Their character traits stand out. This circle of friends has a minimal effect on our own behavior because we do not spend very much quality time with them.

Inner Circle of Friends

- Includes close companions—You regularly talk with them on the phone and exchange text messages.

- These are considered your weekend friends, buddies, maybe even your best friends.

- We choose to spend time with these individuals. They are invited to our social events, such as parties or cookouts, and we may attend other social events with them.

- We have many things in common with these friends, and we enjoy their company.

- We most likely share the major happenings of our lives with these friends.

The people in our Inner Circle of Friends are one step closer to our soul. They will have some effect on our character and who we become because we spend a lot of time with them. We are close enough to share some details of our life with them. A common mistake is to tell secrets to our Inner Circle of Friends. These friends are close to us, but not close enough that we should confide private matters. A sign of maturity is recognizing who is an Inner Friend vs. an Intimate, or Bull's-Eye Friend, and knowing who to open up to fully.

Intimate Circle of Friends (Bull's Eye Friends)

- Includes your best friend (BFF).

- You wholeheartedly trust these people.

- You are soul mates.

- You would lay down your life for these people.

- These friends know you better than you know yourself.

Warning!!! Your Bull's Eye Friends (Intimate Circle) are the individuals that influence you the MOST, and you will undoubtedly find their character traits in your own behavior. Very few people should be allowed here. This area of our lives is limited and restricted to a select few. Choose wisely!

Your Intimate Circle of Friends includes a few people whom we can be vulnerable around and bear our souls, confess our sins, and reveal our secrets, fears, failures, dreams, goals, and personal desires. We know they will never judge us, and they will be there for us no matter what.

Even in spite of our failures, these people will celebrate us, encourage us, and have the permission to correct us. We listen to their advice with an open heart because we trust them completely. They understand us more than any other type of friend.

Again, you must be very wise and cautious about whom these individuals are. You never want to share private, personal, and detailed information with people who are jealous of you, what you have, or who you are. You must discern this and decide.

The Example of Jesus

Jesus Christ shared friendships on all three levels during his earthly ministry. While he loved all human beings, not all of his friendships were equal.

The following diagram illustrates the Circles of Friendship:

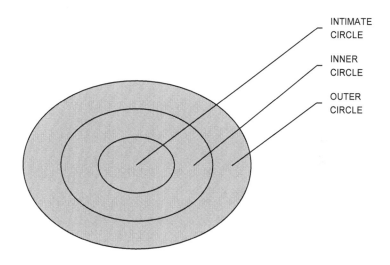

INTIMATE
CIRCLE

INNER
CIRCLE

OUTER
CIRCLE

Jesus' Outer Circle—The Crowds and multitudes

Jesus' Inner Circle—12 Disciples *(Matthew 10:2–4)*

Jesus' Intimate Circle—Peter, James, and John *(Matthew 17:1–3; Luke 8:51–55)*

The point of this chapter is that we must become more aware of the various levels of friends who are in our lives. Some relationships require more work than others. Not everyone can be an Intimate Friend. The closer a friend is to our *'Bull's Eye'*, the more cautious we should be. Be very careful that you do not tell all of your business to the wrong group of people. You must learn to discern the various levels of friendships in your life so that you can properly and effectively fulfill the responsibilities of each.

I encourage you to take a moment to reflect on the friendships in your life. Draw your circle of friendship, and know the company you keep!

Today's Tweet:

@shawnmcbride74

R your friends rowing with u or drilling holes in the boat when U r not looking? #bewareofbadcompany

Chapter 7 Questions for Reflection/Discussion:

1. The Whodini song *Friends* inlcudes the line: *"But, the dictionary doesn't know the meaning of friends."* What is this saying?

2. Think of your Outer Circle of friends. What is a typical conversation you might have with these friends?

3. Now consider your Inner Circle. Are your conversations different with friends in this group?

4. What causes a friend to move from the Outer Circle into the Inner Circle?

5. Few friends make it into a person's Intimate Circle. What qualities do you value most in a super-close best friend?

6. Perhaps you don't have an Intimate Circle. How can you find someone you can fully trust, someone you can be vulnerable with?

7. What happens when you share secrets with someone in your Outer Circle? In your Inner Circle? In your Intimate Circle?

8. Draw your present Circles of Friendship diagram. Now draw your ideal diagram. What is one step you can take to move toward your ideal Circles of Friendship?

Chapter 8
The 7 Characteristics of True Friends

Proverbs 18:24 (NLT)
"There are friends who destroy each other, but
a real friend sticks closer than a brother."

When traveling to the beach from Washington, DC, my family must pass over the incredible Chesapeake Bay Bridge in order to get to Ocean City, Maryland. This is one of the most gorgeous bridges ever constructed!

Using the analogy of a bridge, I want you to consider that friendships are like bridges. A bridge's purpose is to help a driver get from one place to another, just as good friends help us get from one place to another in life. Without bridges on roadways, there would be huge gaps, which we would fall through. Furthermore, a weak bridge may not be able to hold us up and may cause us harm. The same is true of friendships. Having the right kind of bridges (friendships) in our lives, will keep us from falling and help us get to our appropriate destination.

Since friendships are so vital to our success in life, and they have the ability to lift us up, or drag us down, I would like to share with you the qualities you should look for in a friend. Hopefully, you possess some of these same qualities and can offer them to others:

1. Integrity

A true friend has integrity. Integrity means honesty. You know, without a doubt, that this person will always tell you the truth. Integrity also means 'doing the right thing even when nobody is watching.' Therefore, a good friend will respect you (and your wishes) to your face AND behind your back. You can completely trust this person because they keep their promises, keep your secrets, are loyal to you, and love you unconditionally. Their integrity will cause them to protect your reputation. Their integrity is also so deep that they accept you for who you are, including your flaws, failures, mistakes, and sins. Even when you make a fool of yourself, they will know that you only made a mistake.

2. Vulnerable

A true friend is vulnerable with you. To be vulnerable means they voluntarily risk saying something, doing something, or revealing something about themselves, in order to connect with you on a deeper level. This type of friend knows you are not perfect, and as a result, they will expose to you their personal flaws because they rightfully believe that a real friendship is built on unconditional love and acceptance.

3. Humble

A true friend is humble because they are not in competition with you. They accept their weaknesses. They are not SELF-centered, but OTHER-PEOPLE centered. They are at peace with themselves and do not struggle with saying "I'm sorry," or "I made a mistake." These friends do not feel superior over you in the relationship. Therefore, they are able to give you attention when needed, without demanding that you do the same for them.

4. Listens

A true friend listens to you. They have the ability not to just hear what you are saying with your lips, but what you are really saying with your heart. They take the time to understand you. Rather than wanting to be heard, they would much rather listen to you. They are committed to you with a lot of emotional energy. Having a friend who listens to you will deepen your relationship.

5. Sensitive

A true friend is sensitive. Life deals us a variety of situations, but this friend is sensitive to you in a way that is appropriate for the situation and what you are going through at that time. Because they are connected to you beyond a surface level, they genuinely care about you and your feelings. This person has also earned your respect as a source of wisdom. Their advice or constructive criticism is always timely and is given in a way that shows they want to see you improve. Even when it hurts, a real friend will always speak to you in sensitivity that is full of grace and truth.

Proverbs 27:9 (NLT)
"The heartfelt counsel of a friend is as sweet as perfume and incense."

Proverbs 27:6 (NLT)
"Wounds from a sincere friend are better than many kisses from an enemy."

6. Realistic Expectations

A true friend is mature enough to have realistic expectations of you. They know that no friendship is perfect. In other words, they can overlook your shortcomings, extend grace and mercy to you, and ultimately, forgive you.

7. There for You

A true friend is there for you no matter what. They will make themselves available in your time of need, and they are willing to sacrifice their time, effort, and resources to assist you. Regardless of good times or bad, you can count on them to be there for you, physically and emotionally. True friends are also there to set you straight, if they see you going down the wrong path. They will lift you up if they see you falling down. They will also be by your side when everyone else walks out on you.

Job 2:11 (NIV)
"When Job's three friends… heard about all the troubles that had come upon him, they set out from their homes and met together by agreement to go and sympathize with him and comfort him."

Friends are our sunny spot on a cloudy day. They lift us up, cheer us on, cry and hurt with us, and help us navigate life's triumphs and troubles. Life would be no fun without friends to share it with. Make sure you use caution and choose GOOD FRIENDS!

Today's Tweet:

@shawnmcbride74
The Law of Association: U will always become like and reflect the people you hang around the most.
#bewareofbadcompany

Chapter 8 Questions for Reflection/Discussion:

1. Visualize one of your friendships as a bridge. Describe that bridge: Solid or weak? Full of traffic or empty? Well-maintained or falling apart?

2. Have you had a friend talk behind your back? What did you do?

3. It's scary to be vulnerable. How do you know when a relationship is deep enough to expose your personal flaws?

4. Have you seen competition ruin a friendship? How can that be avoided?

5. Most people find it easier to talk than to listen. Come up with two things you can start doing today to be better listener.

6. "Even when it hurts, a real friend will always speak to you in sensitivity that is full of grace and truth." What is your definition of *sensitivity*? *Grace*? *Truth*?

7. Is there a time you regret not being available for a friend? What do you wish you'd done differently?

8. What one friendship characteristic—out of the 7 mentioned—is most important to you?

Chapter 9
Proceed with Caution

Proverbs 12:26 (WEB)
"A righteous man is <u>cautious</u> in friendships."

When exercising with a partner, I have noticed that one of two things always occurs. Either I will adjust to the pace of the person I am walking / running with, or they will adjust to my pace. This happens unconsciously. The people whom you surround yourself with and call your friends in life help determine who you are and who you become. Therefore, I want to encourage and challenge YOU to set the pace in your friendships. Always make sure your friendships stay on a positive path.

Evaluate! Evaluate! Evaluate!

The wise writer of *Proverbs 12:26* reminds us that we must be very cautious when choosing our friends. When we are cautious, we are very attentive to potential problems or dangers that a relationship can have on our well being. A cautious person is extremely careful, reflective, and prudent. They habitually examine the nature of their relationships to ensure they are maintaining a level of healthiness.

Being cautious in choosing your friends is hard work and challenging because you are regularly evaluating the friendships you have, and the new ones you are developing.

My goal in writing this book has been to teach you that your associations are powerful in influencing factors that will eventually shape your character. Many young people I have met and served over the years have been desperate to fit in with their crowd of peers and naïve to the caliber of people around them. Because they are not cautious and, in such, rush to be accepted, many of them began participating in activities they never would have imagined being involved in on their own. But, as part of a larger group of friends, these same activities seemed like acceptable behavior. When you have friends in your life who are bad company, this can be very dangerous and detrimental to your OWN character. Be cautious!

This type of alertness is critical because when people come into our lives, they not only bring their bodies, but their spirits as well. Some people will come into your life as a blessing to help you. Others come into your life as a curse to harm you.

Remember that whenever the Lord wants to BLESS your life, He will always send into your life a PERSON. Whenever the devil wants to DESTROY your life, he will always send into your life a PERSON. Thus, you must discern between the people in your life. You must proceed with caution and ask: What are YOU doing in my life?

One of my favorite subjects in school was math. I still love the process of working with numbers! The following is an example of a mathematical discernment of the people in your life:

1. Who should I <u>ADD</u> to my life?

2. Who should I <u>SUBTRACT</u> from my life?

3. Are certain people <u>DIVIDING</u> me?

4. Which people have helped me <u>MULTIPLY</u> my gifts and talents?

5. What does my life <u>EQUATION</u> look like?

6. Is there <u>EQUIVALENCE</u> in my relationships?

7. Are my relationships an <u>ASSET</u> or a <u>LIABILITY?</u>

Caution! Caution! Caution!

There are three types of people that you should wave your yellow caution flag when you encounter them:

1. Beware of Critical Complainers

Have you ever been around someone whose cup was always half empty, rather than half full? This type of person spews negative energy and can suck all the happiness out of a room in seconds! They can always find fault or something wrong with you, others, and the circumstances of life in general. They are critical of the weather, their parents, their teachers, and practically anyone who has some type of authority over their life.

Complain, complain, complain, and on and on they go! Nothing is ever right for them. Getting closely connected with this type of person will begin to drag you down, especially if you are a positive person. Critical people will begin to infect you and your ways of thinking with their venom that is mostly negative and rarely constructive. If you are not prudent, you will eventually find yourself repeating some of the same negative habits. Remember, no one is immune to bad company. Your view and opinion of others will begin to become skewed.

Scripture warns us of being critical complainers:

Philippians 2:14a (NLT)
"Do everything without complaining and arguing, so that no one can criticize you."

Philippians 2:14–15 (ESV)
"Do all things without grumbling..."

Exodus 16:8 (The Message)
"Moses said, "Since it will be God who gives you meat for your meal in the evening and your fill of bread in the morning, it's God who will have listened to your complaints against him. Who are we in all this? You haven't been

complaining to us—you've been complaining to God!"

James 5:9 (NIV)
"Don't grumble against one another, brothers and sisters…"

1 Peter 4:9 (ESV)
"Show hospitality to one another without grumbling."

2. Beware of Control Freaks

Controlling friends seek to force their opinions and viewpoints upon you, regardless of how you feel. They cause you to lose your personal identity because they want to be in charge and won't allow you to make decisions for yourself. These people bully themselves into your life and expect you to think and act in a way that is acceptable to them and their standards. If you are hanging out with them, they will want to be in control of what movie you see, restaurant you eat at, or activity you participate in, regardless of what you want to do. They constantly want you to surrender to their wishes. This relationship is not a friendship, because friendships are a two-way street. Control freaks are people who must be avoided.

3. Beware of Careless People

Careless people tend to entice and tempt you to do things that you know you should not do. They could 'care less' about the consequences of their actions or yours.

If you are dating someone who tries to entice you to become involved sexually, even though you have made a commitment to abstain, this person is behaving carelessly. They could 'care less' about your character and beliefs, as well as not care about the consequences. This is not a mature person.

A careless person may also encourage you to smoke, get drunk, do drugs, or skip class, regardless of the personal commitments you have made to yourself, or to the Lord. Sometimes, the reason careless people try to encourage you to do things you shouldn't is to make them feel better about themselves for doing it. Be aware of this. Surrounding yourself with this type of person will surely cause your life to crumble and you to become someone you are not proud of. Beware!

Boundaries! Boundaries! Boundaries!

One way you can ensure that you will be cautious and careful in your friendships is by establishing boundaries. Boundaries are like fences. They let us know where we end, and where everyone else picks up. A wise homeowner who has a dog surrounds their home with a fence in order to keep the good in and the bad out. We have to know deep in our heart *who we are*, and *who we want to become*, and then place our fence around that knowledge. We have to have a protective boundary in place to keep the good friends in our life, and the bad friends out of our life.

Today's Tweet:

@shawnmcbride74
If U can't change the people around u, then CHANGE the people around U.
#bewareofbadcompany

Chapter 9 Questions for Reflection / Discussion:

1. How could running alongside another person—a pacesetter—help an athlete in a race?

2. In your friendships, are you typically the pacesetter or the follower?

3. What are the dangers of both the pacesetter and follower?

4. If you recently met someone about your age, what is a yellow caution flag that this might not be a healthy relationship to pursue?

5. Why is it bad to complain? How can a person stop complaining?

6. We all have our opinions, and we often like to share them. Is there a difference between being opinionated and being controlling?

7. Have you had a "care less" friend encourage you to do something you didn't really want to do? How did you handle it?

8. What is one relationship you have right now where you know you need to set up a fence to establish a protective boundary?

Chapter 10
The # 1 Friend You Need: GOD

James 2:23 (NLT)
"Abraham believed God and God counted him
as righteous because of his faith. He was even
called the friend of God."

Throughout our journey, I have tried to give you guidelines to help you make good decisions when choosing your friends. However, it is only fair to let you know that I have not always followed good company. When I was a teenager, I constantly followed the wrong crowd, which led to me making poor choices. I got involved with friends who were dealing drugs. I am ashamed to say that during this period of my young life, I ran several illegal street corner pharmaceutical companies unlike Walgreens, Rite Aid, or CVS.

Unfortunately, due to the pressure and influence of those around me, I chose to smoke weed and drink alcohol to try to escape the emotional pain I was feeling inside my soul. Sadly, I also lost my virginity at a very young age. I deeply regret this decision because it is one that I could never take back.

I lacked a sense of peace in my life. Like many of the people I associated myself with, I was a rebel and was heavily influenced by gangster rap music. I especially had a huge disdain for anyone in authority, particularly my parents, teachers, and law enforcement.

At the age of 17, I came to a point of utter frustration with my sins and myself. My life had no purpose, and I had so many unsatisfied inner needs. This was not what I had envisioned or dreamed for myself. A local pastor shared the gospel with me and told me of God's forgiveness, love, and fulfillment.

Something extraordinary happened to me that year and I was saved. As much sin as I had committed, God still loved me. When I became a friend of God, it was like God filled my deep inner need. Over time, this new relationship began to make a huge difference in my life. It was different than just being religious. I had a real relationship with my creator and I began making decisions in my life that would please Him, rather than my crowd of friends. I also began to become more aware of whom I spent time with. Who knows where I might have ended up, but I am now successful and blessed; thanks be to God!

God is your creator, and He wants to meet your most intimate need for connection. He wants to be your friend. God alone is the ONLY one that can meet ALL your needs, ALL the time. As wonderful as other humans may be, they will eventually fail you in some way. Well-meaning friends, because they are human, will misunderstand you, ignore you, or even forget to do something for you. Only God can fully meet your heart's deepest cries for companionship. I believe that as you draw closer to Him, your need for true friendship will be replaced by a deep, comforting, and life-changing relationship with Him. Why? It's because God helps keep you centered in times of struggle or tribulation. He becomes your rock and comforter so that you do not feel pressured to be accepted by others. Acceptance of God as a friend will change your life for the better. It happened to me. It can happen to you.

In this chapter, you will learn about what it takes to become friends with God: the penalty, the pardon, and God's ultimate promise to us.

Steps to Become a Friend of God
1. The Problem: You Are A Sinner
1 John 1:5 (KJV)
"He is the God of light, and in him is no darkness at all."

The creator of the universe is perfect and holy. God has set laws in place for his creation to obey. They begin with the 10 Commandments. While you might consider yourself a good person compared to most people, how do you measure up against God's law? God's standards for us are much higher than society's standards. For example, have you ever told the smallest lie? Then that would make you a liar:

"For whoever keeps the whole law and yet stumbles at just one point is guilty of breaking all of it." (James 2:10 NIV)

Any disobedience to God is sin. We are all sinners.

Think about these three verses:

Romans 3:23 (NKJV)
"For all have sinned and fall short of the glory of God."

Romans 3:10 (NKJV)
"There is none righteous. No, not one."

Romans 5:12 (NKJV)
"Therefore, just as through one man sin entered the world, and death through sin, and thus death spread to all men, because all sinned."

2. The Penalty: Death
Romans 6:23 (NKJV)
"For the wages of sin is death..."

Disobedience to a holy God deserves a consequence. God shows us His character and laws in His creation—the world around us. He has also written His laws in our hearts and on our conscience. He has also given us His WORD, the Bible. No good judge would let the guilty go free, or the criminal go unpunished.

Neither can a holy, righteous God allow a sinful man to go unpunished. Keep reading, because you are about to learn of our greatest blessing!

3. The Pardon: Jesus Christ Died for Your Sins!

Thankfully, God loves His creation and He has provided a way of escape from the punishment of sin by sending His Son to die in our place. When Jesus died on the cross, it was brutal and he was mocked, spit upon, and cursed. With such love, Jesus died in your place even though he already knew every evil act, word, and thought you would commit. What powerful love! He loves you unconditionally, even to the point of death when you are at your worst.

Consider these three verses:

Romans 5:8 (NKJV)
"But God demonstrates His own love toward us, in that while we were still sinners, Christ died for us."

John 3:16 (NKJV)
"For God so loved the world that He gave His only begotten Son, that whoever believes in Him should not perish, but have everlasting life."

John 15:13–15 (NLT)

"There is no greater love than to lay down one's life for one's friends. You are my friends if you do what I command…Now you are my friends, since I have told you everything the Father told me."

4. The Promise: Your Sins Can Be Forgiven and You Can Have Eternal Life

Sometimes we might think we have to be a better person before God will accept us. Friends, you can never be saved by God by trying to be a good person, nor can you be saved through any amount of good work you perform.

Ephesians 2:8,9 (KJV)

"For by grace have you been saved by faith. And that, not of yourselves. It is the gift of God, not of works. Lest any man should boast."

You and I can be saved only by confessing our sins and placing our faith in God's Son, Jesus Christ, who died and paid for our sins on the cross. We must also surrender our life to His lordship, which places Him in charge of every area of our life. God promises *"To all who received him, to those who believed in his name, he gave the right to become children of God"* (John 1:12 NIV).

Yes, God does hear and accept all who come to put their faith in Him. There is no need to fear death any longer because Jesus broke the power of death on the cross with his own blood. This is such a blessing to us! The price has been paid in full, and it is God's promise to receive all who come to him by placing their faith in Jesus Christ as their Lord and Savior.

Reflect on these two verses:

Romans 10:9–10 (NKJV)
"That if you confess with your mouth the Lord Jesus and believe in your heart that God has raised Him from the dead, you will be saved. For with the heart one believes unto righteousness, and with the mouth confession is made unto salvation."

Romans 10:13 (NKJV)
"For whoever calls on the name of the LORD, shall be saved."

5. Pray the Sinner's Prayer

Just to recap, we are all sinners with a consequence of death, but Jesus Christ, God's only son, died on the cross for our sins. Therefore, God promises that our sins can be forgiven and we can have eternal life. The sinner's prayer is a simple prayer that one prays to God when they understand the magnitude of being a sinner and needing salvation. God is the only one who can save your soul. If you sincerely believe in your heart and you are ready for God to cleanse you of your sins and to have Him in your life, I want to invite you to pray the prayer below at this moment. This prayer is only a guide, but I believe if you are truly sincere and desire to become a friend of God, He will hear you.

Dear God in heaven, I acknowledge to you that I am a sinner, and I am sorry for my sins and the life that I have lived. I need your forgiveness.

I believe in my heart that Jesus Christ died for my sins, and I am now willing to turn from my sin to him for salvation.

At this very moment, I repent of my sins and acknowledge Jesus Christ as the Savior and Lord of my life. I believe.

I humbly ask that you begin to transform my life so that I may bring glory and honor to You alone.

Thank you for giving me eternal life. Amen.

Today's Tweet:

@shawnmcbride74

If God is not in your relationship, you shouldn't be either.

#bewareofbadcompany

Questions for Reflection/Discussion:

1. In just a few words, how would you describe your life up to this point?

2. Do you feel satisfied, or unsatisfied? In peace or turmoil? With purpose, or wandering aimlessly?

3. What role does God play in your daily life?

4. The Bible says every person has sinned. How does God define sin? Do you sin?

5. What is the result of sin *(Romans 6:23)?*

6. Does God love good people more than bad people?

7. What was God's supreme gift to us, as sinners? How do we accept this gift?

8. If you truly want God to transform your life, sincerely read the prayer at the end of the chapter. God hears you. God loves you. Have you made a decision for God to be your best friend?

Conclusion

Be a Thermostat, Not a Thermometer

For many years while speaking to people around the country, I have used a powerful, yet practical, illustration that always causes folks to think deeply about what type of person they are. Sometimes it is easier to understand ourselves if we have a visual. For this lesson, let's think about comparing ourselves to either a thermometer or a thermostat.

A thermometer is a device that tells you how hot or cold a particular environment is. It measures or reflects the temperature, but does nothing to change it. It is a passive device. A thermometer fluctuates depending on the temperature of the area where it's located. Sometimes the mercury moves up and sometimes the mercury moves down and shows that the temperature is cold. It simply reacts by changing itself to the temperature around it.

As it relates to your relationships, I would suggest that you refuse to be a thermometer. What I mean is that you should not allow someone else to dictate YOUR temperature. You should not simply react to the culture around you. Don't sit by and passively allow the negative influences from people around you to harm you. Don't let things 'just happen.'

Thermometer-type people see issues and challenges in their friendships, but they ignore them, or they think there is nothing that can be done about

97

them. They feel helpless as they watch their friends take advantage of them. They act as if they have no power and begin to behave like the company they keep.

A thermostat, unlike a thermometer, sets the temperature in its environment. It controls the temperature. It influences its surroundings. Unlike the passive thermometer, it is an active device.

A thermostat-type person maintains who they are, just as a real thermostat ensures that a given temperature is maintained. In short, they do not change who they are if bad company arrives; they change their company! The people around them are not allowed to change them because thermostat people maintain a level of control over the 'air' *(friends)* around them. When a thermostat-type person is faced with a difficult relationship, they spring into action. They do something. They respond in order to keep the types of friendships they desire.

When I think of a thermostat type of person, four people come to mind: Daniel, Shadrach, Meshach, and Abednego. These are the four young Hebrew men we find in the book of Daniel.
(Daniel, chapters 1–3)

Suffice it to say, these were four young men who refused to live like thermometers in their society. Instead, they chose to live like thermostats. As you read their story, you will learn that they refused to defile themselves and did not give in to the pressure to conform to the world around them. They refused to change their behavior to fit in with the crowd, even when faced with punishment and death. These young men were completely resolved and decided that they would not simply take the temperature of society and move their mercury to match. Instead, they set the temperature in their culture and, ultimately, ended up changing their world.

My hope is that you will take the guidance given throughout this book and use it to help you evaluate the friendships in your life. If you are in negative friendships, work to distance yourself and find more time to develop positive friendships. Know that God is always there to be your #1 friend and to help you along the way.

The **choice** *is yours. Which one will you choose to be…a thermometer or a thermostat?*

Today's Tweet:

@shawnmcbride74
Some people will bless U when they ENTER n2 your life. Others will bless U even more when they EXIT! #bewareofbadcompany

Works Cited

1. Sieving, Renee, et al. "Friends' Influence on Adolescents' First Sexual Intercourse– Perspectives on Sexual and Reproductive Health." *Guttmacher Institute* 38:1 (2007):13–9. Print.
2. Powell, Colin. *My American Journey.* New York: Random House, 1995. Print.
3. Vick, Michael. *Finally Free.* Brentwood, Tennessee: Worthy Publishing, 2012. Print.